D1442418

THE WORLD OF
MIRA ATKESON

A regal old oak tree silhouetted by burnished golden copper colored clouds,
illuminated by late afternoon sun in the hills of Marin County, California.

THE WORLD OF MIRA ATKESON

PHOTOGRAPHY BY MIRA ATKESON, APSA

LITERARY VIGNETTES BY LUELLA O'CONNER

INTRODUCTION BY RAY ATKESON

International Standard Book Number 0-912856-36-X
Library of Congress Catalog Number 77-77012
Copyright© 1977 by publisher • Charles H. Belding
Graphic Arts Center Publishing Co.
2000 N.W. Wilson • Portland, Oregon 97209 • 503/224-7777
Designer • Robert Reynolds
Printer • Graphic Arts Center
Binding • Lincoln & Allen
Printed in the United States of America

The term "world" may be associated with a variety of interpretations by various people. Some confine their "world" primarily to their home. Others may be all wrapped up in their "world" of travel whether it be to the shoreline, mountains, or to foreign lands.

Mira's world had many facets. Her home and family were very important to her and ever since childhood, she was enthralled with the world of beauty she saw in nature. Later as her interests expanded to family and new friends she found enjoyment in service involving people and their interests.

Following our marriage, she adapted her interests and enthusiasm to my world of photography and pursuit of scenic beauty wherever we found it in the mountains and at the seashore, along forest trails and high adventure among the glaciers and peaks of the Cascade Range. With the arrival of our daughter Eleanor, Mira's world was changed for awhile, becoming interwoven with children's interests. It was a natural transition for her to become interested in youth work as the years passed, and she became deeply committed in Campfire Girl activities and organizational work. However, her involvement was directly in line with her interest in that world of beauty to be found in nature. Frequent hikes and camping trips with the girls afforded opportunities for her to share her knowledge and enthusiasm for nature and all that is beautiful in creation.

Mira's early participation in photography was devoted entirely to helping me in my work and accompanying me on countless trips. The help she gave me was immeasurable; moral support when I needed it, patiently waiting with me for desired photo conditions, camping and hiking during unpleasant weather, working in the office after I began my freelance career and often staying home to take care of business when I was away on lengthy assignments or when I was visiting winter resorts for a month or so each year. She suffered with me in adversities and rejoiced when there were reasons for optimism. It was a world of sharing in almost everything with countless concessions on her part.

Eventually she began recording on black and white film with a small folding camera some of the beauty experienced on our trips, and many of the pictures were masterpieces. She even did her own and some of my black and white darkroom processing.

It wasn't until about 1952 that Mira became fully involved in her own world of beauty in color photography. I believe it really started when she, along with Eleanor, and one of her high school friends, took an extensive 6,000 mile trip through Mexico filled with adventure and enjoyment. She took my 35mm Leica camera along and a fascinating travelogue show resulted. From then on the Leica was more in her possession than in mine.

We later joined the Forest Grove Camera Club, a very progressive organization that for years has been one of the nation's most respected. We both enjoyed our association with this group plus membership in the Photographic Society of America which is a world wide organization. It became an amusing sidelight for club members as Mira invariably bested me in our club color slide competition. I finally resorted to use of my larger format cameras exclusively, which eliminated me from that situation.

Mira went on with her pursuit of an expanded world recording its beauties for others to enjoy, and she was rewarded with many medals and awards in club and international competition. She still found time to help me in our expanding office work, plus offering an understanding companionship on our trips, which included several Hawaiian junkets, a trip to Switzerland and Austria. On these trips she recorded vital information for caption material for my pictures. Later, we visited Norway, New Zealand, and Fiji as well as taking excursions to New England in autumn and through the southwestern states in springtime. Of course, all western states, as well as western Canada, had become familiar subjects for our cameras through the years.

It would seem only natural that because of our parallel interests in nature and scenic beauty and our traveling together on the same roads and trails, that duplications of subject and composition would be inevitable.

I frequently marvelled that this seldom occurred. I was, of course, aware that when we were busy taking pictures, Mira went her way and I went mine. Occasionally I might call her attention to some particularly interesting picture subject and she did the same for me. Once in awhile she would take a picture of the same subject, but the results we captured on film rarely came out the same. Actually, there are only three or four pictures within the pages of this book that bear a close resemblance to my photos.

Mira was intensely involved in photographing wild flowers, some of which were almost microscopic in size. She also demonstrated her creative and artistic ability in various innovative forms of photography involving and enhancing the natural beauty of certain subjects.

She frequently expressed her strong opinion that someday there should be a book telling of our photographic experiences, especially featuring some of the unbelievable adversities encountered, often resulting in pictures that got away. Actually I experienced more of those frustrations in pursuit of specific subjects than she did pursuing her hobby. For instance, her 35mm equipment permitted instant action when necessary to capture a fleeting situation of dramatic lighting, or movement that all too often was gone by the time I was able to set up my 4 by 5 on a tripod. I do not mean to imply that her pictures were grab shots or required a minimum of technique. A tripod as well as numerous lenses, filters, and other accessories were an essential part of her working equipment. She worked diligently at her hobby and had her share of personal frustrations, too.

Only photographers who have done a great deal of wild flower photography can be familiar with the patience required in that specialized field. I have done enough of it to be painfully aware of the fact that it is usually more difficult to capture a good flower picture than a striking scenic view.

David Brower of the Sierra Club and Friends of the Earth publication fame once mentioned to me that he liked best the work of photographers who "got their knees wet." Mira surely qualified in that respect. Kneeling and contorting into all imaginable positions necessary so often to catch those beautiful closeups with just the right lighting and background. Sometimes hours were spent clearing distracting background elements and waiting breathlessly for even the slightest breeze to die away which would permit the long stemmed flower to cease its seemingly constant movement.

For many of her flower pictures she used a long lens and visaflex; later, a Nikon with macro, zoom and other lenses were added to her paraphernalia, enabling her to capture closeups and distant subjects with more ease.

Mira occasionally teased me about my animal photography (not one of my specialties). I recall some amusing and interesting shots she took involving animals. In one of those shots she caught me in a pasture beside my camera on a tripod. I was busy searching for a specific filter in a leather pouch attached to my belt while a curious horse with head cocked to one side was seemingly making a close check of my composition through my viewfinder. Another of her pictures taken in Finland caught a reindeer as it went after my handkerchief which protruded from my hip pocket as I was busy endeavoring to photograph other more elusive and distant reindeer in the opposite direction.

One time when we were in the Olympic Rain Forest, I heard her call for me to come to the area where she was taking pictures. I got the impression she had something cornered, but I was too busy to leave the moss covered trees that were the focal point of my camera. I never got around to investigating her problem but sure wished I had done so when she later projected on the screen at home the subject that she had cornered and captured with her camera. That picture will, I'm sure be recognized in this book.

Many of our experiences together on the trail were not amusing. For instance, one September weekend a family of friends accompanied us on a trip to Mt. Rainier for a visit to the Paradise Glacier Ice Caves which were said to be unusually beautiful that year. After hiking up the two mile well-beaten trail, we found that hundreds of other people had also heard the news. The caves were really great and we explored every tunnel and grotto we could find. One huge room was colorful and spectacular with daylight filtering through a scalloped ice ceiling. Unfortunately the weekend crowd made it difficult to do any photography, so Mira and I returned to Mt. Rainier a few days later during the week. The day was unusually clear so I rushed on ahead so as to get a picture of Mt. Adams framed in the cavern entrance. Just as I was entering the cave, several tons of ice came crashing down on the very spot where I would have set my tripod for the Mt. Adams picture.

With some misgivings and thoughtlessness, I went on by the huge pile of ice searching for the hidden tunnel leading to the cathedral-like grotto where we intended to take our photos. Just beyond the small tunnel entrance another and much larger pile of ice had fallen, completely blocking further access in that direction. Fortunately, the small tunnel was off to the side of the larger one, and still intact, so I crawled into the big room which was still beautiful but changed somewhat by other evidence of hazardous conditions that existed.

I finally heard Mira's distant calls and directed her to the palace room. She was almost hysterical as a result of seeing the two great piles of ice under which she feared I might be, a natural reaction that I had failed to consider in the excitement of searching for and finding the room which was our goal for the trip.

After a couple of hours of nerve-tingling photography, we finally left the ice caves with great sighs of relief and several rewarding photos which certainly failed to compensate for the anxiety my thoughtlessness had caused. I have been told that the Park Service has now wisely restricted such freedom of activity when the caves are open for visitation.

Mira had an unhappy magnetic quality or something that attracted mosquitos and other insects like a flower lures bees. Many of her potential pictorial subjects never found their way into the camera because of frequent battles with insects, causing her real agony as well as frustrations. Insect bites usually caused painful swelling which sometimes lasted for days and to add insult to injury, I was comparatively immune, sometimes not even realizing any insects were in the vicinity. She mentioned once that maybe the reason mosquitos usually left me alone was due to something my best friends would not tell me. Anyway, she eventually designed an entire suit of netting which covered her head, limbs, and body. It wasn't the most glamorous attire I've seen, but it surely was the answer to her prayers on wilderness treks.

Yes, Mira did a considerable amount of skiing at Mt. Hood, including climbs to Timberline from Government Camp and back as well as other cross country tours which she enjoyed more than downhill skiing. She also accompanied me a few times to Sun Valley, Idaho; experiences she enjoyed immensely. However, we were not together much on Sun Valley's slopes because I was there for the purpose of taking pictures for my stock files and skied for pleasure only during inclement weather. In fact, on one occasion we were not even roommates because I was a guest of Union Pacific and she was a paying guest of the resort, so she had a lady friend who accompanied us as a roommate while I was living it up in a fine room to myself in the Lodge. Such would have been the case at the other ski resorts, too. Mira wasn't taking pictures seriously until after she chose to discontinue her skiing and mountain climbing activities.

Speaking of mountain climbing, Mira made several climbs to the summit of Mt. Hood once in mid-January. She also climbed both Mt. St. Helens and Mt. Adams a couple of times and explored some of Mt. Hood's glaciers with other climbers and myself. However, her greatest enjoyment was on timbered mountain trails and along the coastline rather than on summit climbs of the high peaks.

Perhaps our favorite field of activity was the coastal area of Oregon in the fall when veiling ground fog frequently hovers over the land and seascapes. We both were enthralled with the sometimes fleeting play of light among fog veiled coastal trees as the sun illuminated a new day, creating countless pictorial effects to be seen and photographed for others to enjoy.

Participating in photography as an amateur gave her maximum pleasure. However, there were numerous times she assisted me with my bookkeeping and eventually all office work. That she loved, too. On two occasions she demonstrated her understanding of my work in the field, for she had closely observed my every move. One time, long before she ever became actually interested in photography I fumbled the ball on an important picture I was assigned to take for an Oil Company calendar. It was a view from an excellent vantage point looking down on the picturesque bridge that spans the mouth of the Rogue River on the southern Oregon Coast. I was scheduled on another assignment which prohibited a return to the bridge in time for another shot to meet the publication deadline. After some last minute instructions from me on the use of the 4 by 5 Speed Graphic I was then using, Mira boarded a bus for Gold Beach where she managed to climb the high hill with the 4 by 5 and heavy tripod, located the vantage point, and returned home with a couple of fine color shots of the bridge.

Several years later she joined a Sierra Club outing in Mt. Assiniboine Park in the heart of the Canadian Rockies. I was unable to make the trip because of participation in the program of the National Convention of Professional Photographers of America which was scheduled for the same period of time. I had a fairly certain market for an Ektacolor negative of Mt. Assiniboine so Mira packed the Rolliflex I then had in addition to her Nikon, lenses and a tripod, for the long hike into the area. Two very outstanding color shots from the 12 exposure roll of film she used were promptly sold. I wish my average of successful commercial pictures were as good.

Being of service in organizational endeavor was another of her enjoyments which helped to pass on to others a greater appreciation of our world of beauty. She gloried in that beauty and was never happier than when she was able to share it with others through the medium of her photography.

RAY ATKESON

Proxy Falls drapes a silvery veil of water over a lava cliff within The Sisters Wilderness in Oregon's central Cascade Range.

Anemone seed pods often called "Old Man of the Mountain", highlighted by
bright sunshine, photographed in Mt. Rainier National Park, Washington,
with the serrated Tatoosh Range in the background.

A nesting Eider duck ignores her wild instincts as she protects her eggs on the shoreline of a fjord in northern Norway. Norwegians gather Eider down from countless nests after the ducklings have hatched and gone their way.

Avalanche lily is one of the most delicate of mountain flowers, often growing
on the edge of snow fields. Mira captured this striking picture with
the sun almost directly behind the bloom.

Salmon Fishermen on Tillamook Bay greet the rising sun as it breaks over the
Coast Range of Oregon.

One of Mira's experimental photos of an azalea blossom releasing bubbles
after being submersed in a glass bowl of water.

Come out I thought,
and walk with me,
the breeze is up,
and it wafts the sea.
We'll cross the beach,
to the sandy bar,
when the tide is out,
we can go quite far.

Tonight I sit on a dramatic shore,
of molten silver,
and watch the sea gulls soar,
while the breakers roll in from the sea
And lonely I wish for,
your company.

Sunlight casts a metallic gleam across Pacific surf beneath leaden gray clouds
on Washington's Olympic Peninsula.

Pacific breakers illuminated by low sunlight as they roll in on California's
Monterey Peninsula.

Colorful columbine blossoms and buds sway on a long graceful
stem in Oregon. Over 70 species of this flower are found in the Northern
Hemisphere.

A tide water home on the banks of the Siuslaw River near the community of
Florence along the Oregon Coast.

One of several geologically ancient buttes in central Oregon's Ochoco region
adds its touch of symmetric interest to this photo of nostalgic autumn beauty.

A huge Pacific breaker explodes against the Na Pali cliffs of Kauai Island,
Hawaii, during a tropical storm.

Giant redwoods reach high into the fog in Redwood National Park, near the northern California coastline.

Ryhthmic designs woven by a combine harvester in a Wasco County grain
field in north-central Oregon

Picturesque oak trees in southern California's Santa Ynez Valley are shaped
and sculptured by prevailing winds which flow inland from the Pacific.

A forest fire of Vine Maple leaves,
illuminate the deep shade,
of a rainy day,
and emblazons its signature,
across the forest floor,
under the tall green giants,
of Oregon.
Leaves that dance their way
to the summit ridge,
and lift their arms in supplication.
A supplication for continued rain.
Leaves that understand the gravity
of a long parched summer,
and tilt their faces to quaff
the refreshing liquid affection
so desperately needed
at summers' end.

Flaming colors of autumn on surface of vine maple foliage contrast
dramatically with an evergreen forest photographed on a rainy day in Oregon's
central Cascade Range.

Tule Lake National Wildlife Refuge in northern California is a rendezvous
for about 8,000,000 migrating waterfowl during autumn months.
Mira's camera seems to have caught a good percentage of them in evening
flight. Mt. Shasta reaches over 14,000 feet toward the cloud filled sky on
the distant horizon.

Brilliant sunlight rims the wing feathers of a gull lazily soaring in the clear
blue sky along the Washington Coast.

Palm trees sway in the evening breeze on the Kaanapali coast of Maui as a
glorious sunset spreads vivid colors across the clouds above.

Storm clouds melt beneath brilliant sunlight which illuminates mists rising
against 4,000 foot mountains of the Na Pali Coastline as turbulent surf lashes
the precipitous cliffs of Kauai Island, Hawaii.

A young mountain stream tumbling down a flower fringed stairway of rock ledges in Mt. Rainier National Park, Washington.

Spirelike alpine firs are silhouetted by hovering clouds in the valley of the
Suiattle River in Washington's Glacier Peak Wilderness.

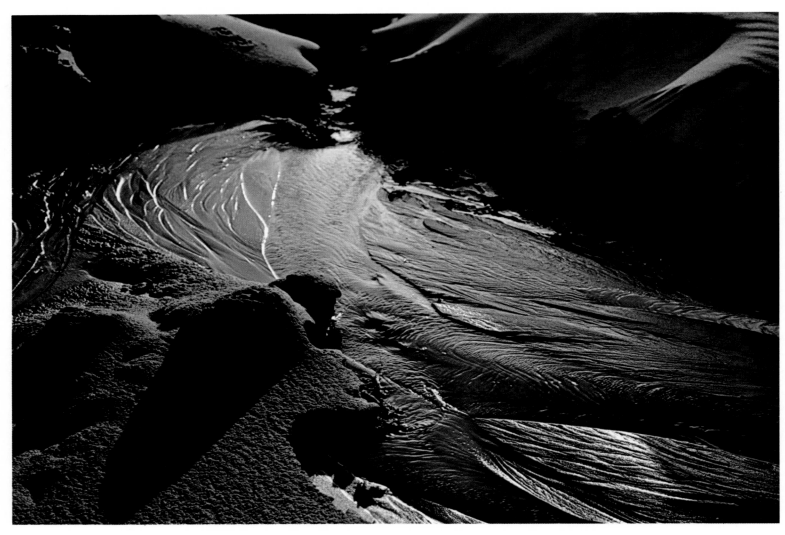

The vast area of sand dunes in Oregon Dunes National Recreation Area on
the central Oregon Coast is unique in that the dunes rest on a plentiful supply
of water. Many lakes and island projections dot the seemingly endless dunes.
Springs, like this one gleaming in sunlight, flow from the sand into some of the
lakes or disappear beneath a neighboring dune.

This creature captured by Mira in the Olympic Rain Forest was just cause for excitement when she discovered a fallen tree draped with a blanket of moss as only nature could render the end result.

Crown Point reflects warm colors of day's end as dark clouds shade the
Columbia River Gorge.

Picturesque outdoor light beams a cheery welcome for visitors as new snow
mantles the winter world in the high residential hills skirting Portland, Oregon.

Listen to a child,
and it will teach you something
of love and faith and wonder.
The sweetest way to see the world,
is reflected in the eyes of a child.

Wonderment of the world,
let my treasures through;
I like watching you.

"Rain comes easy, doesn't it mommy.
Look how the little tiny raindrops
hang on tight
like they're afraid they're going to fall.
It's so far down to the ground,
no wonder they're scared.

Look how they reach out and hold hands,
to make one big drop,
that hangs by its' tail.
And when it gets so heavy,
that it can't hang any more
it wig-wags like polywogs do,
to our window sill.

Our young granddaughter became enthralled as she traced raindrops
streaming down the window glass.

Offshore rocky pinnacles thrust through a blanket of low-lying fog and surf at the foot of coastal mountains along the Oregon Coast.

A graceful palm tree, symbol of the Hawaiian Islands, arches out over Opehikao point which is one of the most photogenic settings on the "big island," Hawaii.

An old deserted ranch building and windmill silhouetted by afternoon
sunlight and clouds in Harney County, Oregon.

In Oregon's rangeland east of the Cascades, the Tygh Valley all-Indian rodeo
lures cowboys and spectators for a two-day event each spring.

Fog adds a challenge and intrigue to entice two hikers exploring the Alpine
wonders of Washington's Glacier Peak Wilderness.

The tiny Swiss village of Findeln clings to a steep mountain slope far below
the towering peak of The Matterhorn. The cloud banner is a frequent added
attraction of this famed peak.

Sunset tinted clouds silhouette The Needles towering above the surf-washed sands of Cannon Beach on the Oregon Coast.

A contrasting environment of sweet peas blooming beside a weathered and
deserted mountain home in western Oregon.

Sunset glow tints the clouds hovering over snow-sprinkled wheat fields on
a southeastern Washington ranch.

Shooting Star, also known as Bird Bill, is one of the most interesting and photogenic of western wild flowers. Mira took this photo in an alpine meadow in the Cascade Range.

49

Trout Lake Creek cascades down a rocky slope fringed with colorful foliage of cottonwoods near Mt. Adams, Washington.

Birch trees, sumac and other shrubs create a kaleidoscope of fantastic color
for New Englanders each autumn season which lures photographers and
nature lovers from all over the world.

December embroidered our holly tree,
in hoarfrost bright,
the hours I lay asleep last night.
Who needs to covet jets and jewels,
of queens in rusty crowns,
when through their windows
skylights dance,
on trees in frosty gowns.

I like a tree like that.
A tree that is old when I am born
and young when I am old.
A tree with splintered sunlight on it.
A tree of fire and ice.

Hoarfrost rims holly foliage in western Oregon. Old English holly thrives in the mild climate and fertile soil of the Willamette Valley.

Cattle have returned from their high summer rangeland to spend autumn and
winter seasons in the beautiful John Day Valley of Oregon

Mt. Adams, ringed by a lei of low clouds, looks down on a wheat ranch in
southern Washington's Klickitat Valley. Mt. Adams is second only to Mt.
Rainier in height and size, dominating the lower ridges of the Cascade Range.

Monument to the past. This picturesque old ghost snag on the Monterey Peninsula has finally become a casualty of Pacific storms. It no longer stands defiantly on this rocky perch above the sea.

An offshore breeze unfurls spindrift from the crest of a Pacific breaker as it races toward Oregon coastline at Ecola State Park. Haystack Rock and other pinnacles are silhouetted by moisture haze rising from the surf.

One of many outstanding pictures Mira took on a Sierra Club outing in Mt. Assiniboine Park in the Canadian Rockies. The area is reached by many miles of hiking and this scene was one that rewarded members of the outing when they climbed one of the peaks overlooking glaciers and lakes of the region.

One of several photos Mira and I took of changing cloud formations off the
Oregon Coast as sunlight beamed on Pacific surf below. (This illustration is
repeated on jacket.)

Early morning mists hover over Lake Matheson at the base of Mt. Cook Range
in New Zealand. Here, the eye climbs from sea level to the 12,000 foot elevation
of the mountain crests.

The golden globe flower, apparently a member of the buttercup family,
dominates a field of varied wild flowers on gentle slopes in the upper reaches
of the Swiss Alps.

Snow-capped peaks tower above a picturesque Church at Olden, Norway,
land of many fjords and magnificent mountains.

In Austria's Lakes Region, a lush crop of hay has been cut by scythe, then draped over wooden frames to cure. The resulting design created an illusion of penguins following their leader up the hillside to a picturesque chalet on the edge of the forest.

A lone cow wandering toward the welcome shelter of farm buildings in
southern Washington's Klickitat Valley.

A few ducks ascend from the golden sunset tinted waters of Tule Lake
National Wildlife Refuge in northern California. Millions of waterfowl
rendezvous here during their annual autumn migration to southland
winter feeding grounds.

Our rain never crashes, it caresses. When you
tilt your face skyward it kisses your forehead
as soft as a whisper. Its melodic tinkle comes on
little silver feet.

Somehow a diamond seems less grand when held next
to the scintillating liquid gems. A proud parent
nimbostratus cloud beams its applause through
such dazzling perfection, (and so do I).

Raindrops hanging on a window glass are transformed into sparkling beauty
as sunlight finds its way through springtime clouds.

A lenticular cloud hovers over Mt. Rainier, Washington as moisture-laden winds from the Pacific are condensed by cold air currents rising from the glacier crowned dome of the great mountain. Mountaineers know that Mt. Rainier creates its own weather and such cloud caps often indicate approaching storms.

Smoke from a smoldering fire produced this unusual effect, which Mira
captured, at the Sol-duc shelter in the Olympic Rain Forest.

Haze veiling the Wetterhorn silhouettes a beautiful church in Grindewald, the heart of Switzerland's Bernese Oberland region.

A beautiful autumn day experienced in northern Idaho overlooking Coeur
D'Alene Lake and cottonwood trees bordering the St. Joe River which flows
far out into the lake.

The Jungfraujoch is high above the clouds and the rest of the world on the
crest of the Swiss Alps. A cog railway climbs up the steep glacier clad slopes
to 11,000 feet traversing directly through a mountain tunnel for many miles.
Mira and I spent four strenuous hours of climbing and taking pictures in this
exciting high mountain world above the 11,000 foot level.

Comparatively warm air currents flow beneath Paradise Glacier on Mt.
Rainier sculpturing the ancient ice into fantasy grottos and palace rooms.
Translucent light from outside the caverns filters through the thin ceiling.

North Head Lighthouse flashes a warning from its lofty point on the southern
Washington Coast high above the Pacific.
The beauty of this picture resulted from sandwiching a very ordinary
transparency of the lighthouse with a colorful cloud transparency as a
background.

Mira took this Rain Forest photo in Olympic National Park. Adverse weather actually is favorable for forest pictures which might be much less successful if captured in sunlight and shadows of a clear day.

Twin arches of an ancient Roman stone bridge spans a clear mountain stream in Valley Verzasca in southern Switzerland. This unique foot bridge is in continuous use and attracts thousands of visitors interested in its beauty and historical significance.

Spreading boughs of a regal maple tree unfold a canopy of golden autumn tinted foliage over a stone fence that may have been here since colonial days in New England.

An indigo ribbon of water,
its satin unfurled,
slides through the hush
of my marshmallow world.

Yesterday's branches naked and bare,
wear puffs of cotton in their hair.
It had been barren, dark and bleak,
and now its beauty none can speak.

I hesitate my feet to trod
lest they should mar
the robe of God.

The Santiam River flows swiftly through a winter fairyland in the foothills of Oregon's central Cascade Range.

Spruce trees partially frame an intriguing vista of coastal mountains rising
above fog-veiled Pacific surf at Cape Meares, Oregon.

Frost whitens a forest road which has been sprinkled with leaves from autumn colored aspens in the Uinta Mountains, northern Utah.

Late afternoon sunlight breaks through clouds to cast a warm glow on
colorful sandstone cliffs of Cape Kiwanda and Pacific surf on the
Oregon Coast.

Indian paint brush, usually considered to be a flower, actually becomes a summer showpiece of nature as a result of foliage coloration. It generally occurs in bright red or scarlet colors.

An early autumn snow fall draped over Mt. Sneffels and golden aspen foliage
at Dallas Divide in southwestern Colorado.

A shaft of sunlight pierces early morning coastal ground fog to illuminate an inviting woodland trail in Oregon's Cape Lookout State Park.

Rhododendrons flourish and bloom in colorful profusion on the shadowed
floor of giant coastal redwood groves in Redwood National Park, California.

The wild Owyhee River races through a spectacular and colorful gorge in
eastern Oregon. It is one of the west's most challenging and scenic rivers
luring numerous white water boaters to adventure during late spring
and early summer months.

A heavy autumn snow fall blankets valley meadows and mountain slopes of southwestern Colorado.

Sunlight illuminates a swirl of fronds of a beautiful tree fern in the rain forests
of Westland National Park, New Zealand.

An abandoned cabin in a grove of autumn-colored cottonwoods
in central Utah.

Graceful curves carved in the soil by a wheat drill reach out across grain land in eastern Idaho. In the background are towering peaks of the Teton Range in the northwest area of Wyoming.

Dew drops on the webs have strung,
a galaxy of lace.
Hurry while the dawn is young,
come and see this grace.

A cascade of melodious bird song
from the branches rise.
These are the things that feed my soul,
the beauty that I prize.

A spider web in marshy area near Lewis and Clark National Memorial
sparkles with jeweled droplets of dew as morning sunlight awakens a new
day on the Oregon Coast.

This setting of serenity and alpine grandeur provides an ideal place for rest and meditation for a venerable Swiss oldster.

A picturesque summer home nestled in a forest of larch and pine trees on the
shore of a lake in northeastern Washington. The larch (often called tamarack)
loses its needles for the winter season, but stages a spectacular show of
autumn color before the needles drop.

Sunlight breaks through winter storm clouds to spotlight turbulent Pacific surf
churning its way shoreward at Ecola State Park, Oregon.

The Snake River flows out of cloud-shadowed Jackson Hole, Wyoming into a spot of sunshine creating a dramatic contrast of mood as it illuminates foreground grass and foliage.

New England is justly famed as the autumn showcase of America. Colorful
settings will reward natives and visitors at nearly every turn of the road.

A Norwegian mountain stream cascades through a birch forest corridor
enroute to its rendezvous with a Scandinavian fjord.

A small herd of Hereford cattle graze and rest contentedly beneath the spreading boughs of an old oak tree in a lush green California pasture.

Mitre Peak and hovering cloud tufts mirrored on tranquil tide water of Milford
Sound in New Zealand. This six thousand foot peak rising directly from sea
level of the sound is the most famous landmark in the country.

Turbulent Pacific surf dances and leaps around the defiant spire of Rampart
Rock off the Oregon Coast.

The setting sun silhouettes seagulls as they soar over a surf-washed beach on the Washington Coast.

Ice falls of several glaciers tumble down into the 14-mile-long Aletsch Glacier
on the crest of the Swiss Alps.

A colorful rose blooming in a home garden in Portland, Oregon,
"The Rose City". This city of trees and roses and open spaces has six major
parks totaling 7200 acres.

Sheep graze contentedly in a meadow of Pleasant Valley at the foot of the lofty San Juans and Mt. Sneffels in southwestern Colorado.

A duck briefly leaves her young brood to enjoy the relaxation of an
exhilarating stretch of wings and legs.

I am sustained,
in soul and mind,
by the ecstacies of autumn,
for all mankind.

Her giant scotch tartan muffler,
of russet, green and gold,
stretched out . . . . .
all along the river,
for as far as eyes can behold.
Flamboyant October leaves,
whorling as they fall,
don't you love the quiet things,
that make no noise at all.

Clear blue waters of the Snake River contrast dramatically with brilliant
orange foliage of cottonwoods along its banks where the river leaves Jackson Hole,
Wyoming enroute to Idaho.

109

Sheep graze at the base of the eastern foothills in Oregon's Coast Range.
This pastureland lies approximately due west of Corvallis.

Vertical cliffs and lofty, glacier-clad mountain peaks of the Swiss Alps reach to
the clouds thousands of feet above the beautiful Lauterbrunnen Valley in the
Bernese Oberland region of Switzerland.

Up high in the Sierra,
up beyond traffic dins'
dirty constant groan,
your conifers stand patiently waiting,
awaiting you, to *hear* their home.
Listen to the quiet,
and you will hear,
the Minarets' awesome aria,
of ringing silence,
echoing in your ear.

Serrated crags of the Minarets in California's Minarets Wilderness scrape the
clouds above veiled foothills of the Sierra Nevada Range.

Deer on Hurricane Ridge in Olympic National park are accustomed to human visitors entering their domain and photographers frequently find opportunities to photograph the deer in their natural habitat.

A 28 mm lens and a polarizing filter dramatized a fantastic cloud formation as it moved across the sky above Mt. Jefferson in Oregon's Cascade Range.

Mt. Hood's lofty volcanic cone shrouded by Indian Summer haze towers high
above a picturesque ranch in the hills above The Dalles, Oregon.

A sunburst shoots colorful rays through spruce boughs and early morning fog in the Tillamook Valley on the Oregon Coast. One of the comparatively few scenes so dramatic that both Mira and I couldn't resist duplicating the picture.

Golden autumn-tinted leaves decorating white-barked aspen trees in Swan Valley, Idaho; dramatized by use of a Polaroid filter.

The sun flashes a spotlight through rain clouds at the precise moment to catch
a capricious cloud playing on a steep mountainside above Milford Sound, on
the South Island, New Zealand.

Golden poppies sprinkled over a grassy knoll crowned by a wind sculptured
oak tree in Marin County, California.